# SURGE:

## The CEOs Guide to Baggage Free Success

## Jamella Stroud

SURGE: The CEO Guide To Baggage Free Success
Copyright © 2018 by Jamella Stroud. All rights reserved.
All rights reserved.

No part of this publication may be reproduce, stored in a retrieval system or transmitted in any way by means, electronic,
mechanical, photocopy, recording or otherwise without the prior written
permission of the author except as provided by USA copyright law.

Cover image designed copyright © Brand It Beautifully All rights reserved.
Author photo copyright © 2018 by Michele Moore All rights reserved.
Edited by Monique Nixon

ISBN: 9781790396849

Author's Note: The Twelve Steps are mentioned of Alcoholics Anonymous. Mentioning the Twelve Steps does not mean that Alcoholics Anonymous has reviewed or approved the content of this publication or that AA agrees with the views expressed herein. The views expressed here are solely those of the author. The views expressed in this book do not promote AA or any Twelve Step program.

This book is dedicated to the employees at my first company J'S Tax Service, LLC with respect, love, and thanksgiving, I write. I learned so many lessons and I thank you all for being a part of my progress and process.

"You can have financial success without God, but you can't have significance, there is no significance to any process that God is not the center of. There may be short term success an illusion of happiness, but no deep seated fulfillment in any process where God is not the center."

~ Steven Furtick

# CONTENTS

**INTRODUCING** CONFESSIONS OF A CONTROL FREAK ....... 1

**CHAPTER 1** ACKNOWLEDGE .................................................. 27

**CHAPTER 2** BELIEVE ................................................................ 32

**CHAPTER 3** CHOOSE ............................................................... 38

**CHAPTER 4** INVENTORY ......................................................... 45

**CHAPTER 5** ADMIT .................................................................. 54

**CHAPTER 6** WILLING & READY ............................................. 60

**CHAPTER 7** ASK ....................................................................... 66

**CHAPTER 8** WILLING TO AMEND ......................................... 71

**CHAPTER 9** AMENDS ............................................................... 79

**CHAPTER 10** CONTINUE ......................................................... 85

**CHAPTER 11** SEEK .................................................................... 91

**CHAPTER 12** AWAKENING .................................................... 100

**ACKNOWLEDGEMENTS** ....................................................... 107

> "The life of the control freak is always the same. There is no excitement, no glamour, no fun. There are no good times, there is no joy, there is no happiness. There is no future and no escape. There is only an obsession. An all-encompassing, fully enveloping, completely overwhelming obsession."
>
> James Frey

# INTRODUCING

# CONFESSIONS OF A CONTROL FREAK

**"When you try to control everything you enjoy, honor, accept nothing." -Jamella Stroud**

## MY LIFE

I was born and raised in Birmingham, The Magic City, and I must say my story is truly magical to say the least. I grew up in the inner city and life was fun. I played outside all day in the summertime only coming in due to thirst and bathroom breaks. I lived the normal inner city kids life.

Growing up, I was fortunate to have an opportunity to see outside my reality and life in the city due to frequent trips to Dallas/Fort Worth, TX where I would go some summers to visit my uncle who was an entrepreneur. Visiting Texas seeing and experiencing his lifestyle captivated me and I knew I would someday be an entrepreneur. I desired to live the life I saw that was totally different from my daily inner city life.

Surprisingly, my first introduction to entrepreneurship was from my father and mother who were pharmaceutical sales reps; however, they didn't work for the pharmaceutical companies, they worked for themselves. I hope you know where I'm going with this, yes, my parents were drug dealers. They had a whole company, or so the stories I've heard. Believe it or not, there's a lot of correlations to that and entrepreneurship. They had amazing skills that when turned for good, made them amazing people. Although I believed they were amazing then, they were survivors doing the best they could with the information they had at the time. Some of the skills they possessed included team building skills because they knew the value of having a team to fulfill the dream. This also included people and sales skills as they understood the importance of being a people magnet and the value of getting people to know, like, and trust them. They valued work ethic. My parents were hard workers and believed they had to do what they had to do to pay the bills.

Okay, let's get back to me, I started my journey as an entrepreneur at a very early age; six to be exact.. My mother was a single parent and did what was needed to make the ends meet, so she became the neighborhood, or the project's, "candy lady." We had a real store in our kitchen! My mother had a brass rack in the kitchen that displayed all the candy she sold. When my mother was at work, it was our responsibility to manage the candy store and sell candy to the customers. We did very well as we handled the money and handed out candy to our friends and neighbors. We became little sales reps!

My journey into sales continued through my high school years. My mother went from selling candy to selling candy apples, and once again, I was her saleswoman. I would pack my backpack full of apples before I embarked upon my one mile trek to school. I was eager to sell the candy apples, and I wasn't shy about asking students to buy my apples. I was good at sales, period. I would increase the price by a quarter to increase my profit margin with the sales. I would take all the money home to my mother and she would pay me my agreed earnings plus an additional amount. I was excited as I continued to sell for the rest of my high school years.

After I finished high school, I went to college but left halfway through the second semester and later found out I was pregnant with my daughter. I gave birth to her at the age of twenty, and at the age of 23, her father passed and this tragic event officially made me a single mother. I had to figure out how to take care of myself and my daughter so I did what I had to do to survive. I didn't become a pharmaceutical sales rep like my parents, but I did sell knockoff handbags while working as a shampoo tech at my friends salon, and I also used my checking account and wrote worthless checks from it to pay the bills. Somehow during all my struggles, I managed to graduate from college thanks to federal programs like Workforce Initiative Act, (WIA), Food stamps, and Section 8. These were all services that I utilized once upon a time while in college.

At the age of twenty-six, I started my first traditional business as a seasonal tax preparer for J'S Tax Service before later becoming an Enrolled Agent. My first office was actually housed inside the salon I worked for. I had a dream to start the business, I went to training and got a certification before borrowing three-hundred and fifty dollars from my mother. I also applied for an Office Depot credit card which was approved for one thousand dollars. I then purchased the tax software with the money from my mother, and also purchased laptop, printer, paper, etc., with the office depot card. I began to tell people in the salon what I was doing and my efforts and faith paid off. I took all the profits from the first season reinvested and the second year opened a storefront, having five employees, including an office manager "the rainmaker" assistant, receptionist, and other staff. Before we get too deep into this story, let's talk about me being a control freak.

## SHE'S GOTTA HAVE IT

I have a confession. I'm a recovering control freak. The truth is, I wanted to control every aspect of my life and the lives of those around me. I wanted things to be just like I imagined them to be in my head. My employees had to act as I instructed them without questioning me. If they didn't do as I stated, I reprimanded them by reducing their hours or abruptly removing them from the schedule. When things changed, I didn't know how to handle it. I lost control- screaming, yelling, belittling, dismissing, and minimizing the efforts of others. I lived and believed the quote "If you want something done right, you have to do it yourself." I'm not sure who said this, but I'm sure he/she was a control freak. When those whom I interviewed, trained and hired didn't do things "right" according to my standards, that were ever-changing, I would go behind them, criticize them and do it myself. I was incapable of seeing my errors, apologizing, or being vulnerable, I was emotionally unintelligent. I was business and all business only focusing on results, by any means necessary even if those means diminished my staff and the people who cared about me the most. I gossiped about my staff saying things like, "they are incompetent, inadequate" to do the job they were hired for after hiring them. I didn't allow them to fully function in the area which they were experts. I wanted them to do what I said, as I said, as ever changing as I said it. I was the "BOSS", "HNIC", (Head Nigga In Charge) and I wanted everyone to know it without a doubt because it was a dictatorship working for me and not a democracy. My voice, thoughts, beliefs, and ideas mattered the most in the business. I was a control freak.

Now, I'm a recovering control freak. I've been a

recovering control freak since 2013, and it has been the best choice I've made in my life.

Control was the symptom the thing that came to the surface, but I had deeper issues that laid dormant, and that was the real issue, along with anyone else who was a control freak. I was obsessive- compulsive, angry, passive-aggressive, anxious and afraid. I feared losing control. No, I didn't just wake up one morning and decided I was going to be a control freak. I had years of unprocessed and unreleased baggage that was the cause of the controlling behavior. The years of unreleased baggage began to compound like compounding interest, it stacked up. Unlike compounding interest, compounding baggage is has a negative effect instead of a positive one on relationships of all kind.

Let's explore what was really under the surface of the controlling behavior.

To fully understand the controlling behavior, you need to understand me. For you to understand me, you will need to know other parts of my childhood story.

At the age of six my paternal grandfather died of heart failure. I was shocked, confused and didn't understand what happened. My family didn't sit me down and have a conversation with me about what that meant for me. I was left to figure out the emotional impact of this experiment by myself.

At the age of eight, I was molested. I didn't tell any adults about what happened to me. The experiences began happening within the confines of my family a male and female cousin and male uncle. Later it extended to others outside my family. I carried the experiences throughout my young adult life before I told a soul, therefore I was left to figure out and deal with the impact of yet again another experience by myself. I share a more in depth experience in my book, *Bulimic To Believer.*

During the time the molestation started, my father experienced a life-threatening and life altering experience; he was shot in the stomach. This experience almost left him dead, but thanks be to God through the hand of the physicians he lived, and I again was left to my own devices to cope with the traumatic experience.

I became promiscuous, which was a byproduct of the molestation, and at the age of thirteen, was exposed to a non-life threatening sexual transmitted infection.

I was very aggressive during my tender years of

fourteen through sixteen. I was angry with my story and didn't know a healthy way to process the pain of the experiences. I fought as a way to express my anger and my tenth grade year of high school I got into a physical altercation which left me with a scar on my lips as I was cut during the fight. I still hadn't learned to express the pain of my experiences and found myself in a verbally and emotionally abusive relationship at the age of eighteen with my daughter's father, who was also an alcoholic.

When I was nineteen, I became pregnant with my daughter, who changed the trajectory of my life. At the age of twenty, I was now faced with being a single mother who still I hadn't released her heavy baggage. The emotional pain from all my childhood experiences were still within me. They didn't go anywhere they continued to compound and the baggage continued to build and build.

At the age of twenty-one, I wanted out. I was tired of the emotional pain of my story. I needed to release the baggage. I would have done anything at that time for relief! I decided to lose weight but little did I know I would me be introduced to a coping mechanism that only proved valuable for a short time. I was determined to lose weight, I believed I would be better if I did, and did it quickly. As with any slippery slope I began binging and purging, over exercising, and abusing laxatives. I developed an eating disorder to cope with the unreleased psychological baggage. Life was spiraling out of control, not only was I a mother, having to care for another life, but I still hadn't quite mastered the art of living my own life.

Although I was a single mother, that didn't stop me from enrolling in college at the age of twenty-two. I was determined to do something meaningful, something different with my life despite my experiences and the unprocessed baggage. I enrolled with the eating disorder and other life issues, yet my life was still unmanageable. Although I appeared to be a functioning, successful young woman on the outside, my insides were lifeless under the weight of raw feelings, thoughts, and undigested emotions.

Life continued to spiral downwards for me. At the age of twenty-three, my daughter's father died. I was still a college student and I still needed to make ends meet so I began to work at a salon as a shampoo assistant. I sold "knock-off "handbags from the salon I worked for, and I wrote checks from my account that was short lived. The eating disorder behavior increased as life became more and more unmanageable. Upon graduation at twenty-six, I became a full-time entrepreneur still carrying all the baggage from my childhood, eating disorder, and controlling behavior as my cover up. I accomplished all of these things in life without processing a single negative emotion. They continued to be buried in my thoughts. I didn't seek counseling or speak with anyone about the truth of my story. I was running a business and leading my employees with the unrefined weight and burdens, or shall I say emotional un-intelligence. I felt out of control. If truth be told many of the experiences were out of my control. The molestation was directly connected to the need for control over everything. I was powerless because of those experiences as my body and choice were dominated by someone else and from that experience, they had power over my body, mind, and even my behavior. Now that you understand my back story and how I became a control freak, let's explore how it impacted me in business and other areas of life.

## CONFESSIONS

The bulimia was connected to the molestation. It was the thing or place I felt most in control. I had a choice and say over what happened to my body; what I ate, how much I ate, and when it would be purged or released from my body. It was indeed a slippery slope, and one that I couldn't control after a while because it controlled me. The occasional binge and purging turned into a daily binge and purge. I exercised and then abused laxatives. The slope was quick and fast. I was totally powerless but continued to present myself to be normal and okay to those around me.

Once in business, I willed myself into stopping the behavior without therapeutic help or intervention. I was the equivalent to a "dry drunk." A "dry drunk" is explained in the sober environment as person who no longer drinks or uses drugs but continues to display and behave in the same dysfunctional ways. Another definition of a "dry drunk", is a person whose mindset and emotional Intelligence has not been transformed after stopping the addictive behavior. The behaviors of bulimia, such as binging and purging, were not present, but all of the effects control, fear, shame, and ultimately the mindset, was still there. I was leading my employees with this deadweight, and the baggage was impacting my relationships, family, friends, employees and my capacity to effectively lead, live and love those around me in and out of business.

The third year in business, my sister began to work for me as the office manager. She came from a very reputable company in corporate America. She brought a lot of insight and information to offer as it related to the operations of my business, not to mention she also has a degree in Business Management. One day I gave her a task of which she was very capable of performing. I slowly approached her desk and stood ominously over her shoulder watching her perform the assigned task. I firmly stated in a passive aggressive tone, "You should change that font to a different one and move the first paragraph up." My sister turned around quickly in her chair and looked me directly in my eyes before she replied, " I understand this is your business; however, what you're not going to do is micromanage me. You gave me a job to do and I'm going to do it. If you would like to do it yourself you can go right ahead, but I will not be micromanaged." I paused as her words pierced my body like an electric current went from my head to my toes. I was very grateful for her assertiveness that day. I listened. said, "Okay," and walked away. At that moment I realized she caused me to confront and attend to the inner control freak that lived without shame inside of me.

There was another interaction with the other office manager, or "Rainmaker", as we so affectionately called her. She was an amazingingly talented, people person who didn't meet a stranger. This office manager was eager to learn, ambitious, and determined to do her best. Although she was a different hue than me, we had a lot of similarities personally. She was the key employee bringing in new business all the time while supporting the businesses growth and expansion. I continued to spiral out of control internally becoming greedy and overzealous because I wanted more for me. I wanted more power, control, and more money. I wanted more, and the only way I believed I could achieve that was reducing the pay of the "Rainmaker." Let's be clear during this time, I was totally unconscious of my behavior and the underlying issues that supported them.

One winter morning while at the office. I called her into the conference room to explain my " strategic business move". We sat at the oval conference table where I confidently pulled out my legal pad that had all the details of the pay changes I was proposing. With excitement in my voice, I explained my proposal to eliminate her commission and just paying her a salary . She was making twenty percent commission from every return she prepared and a weekly salary. There was great potential for her to bring home well over a thousand dollars weekly. My new strategy was to only pay her a weekly salary that was more than her salary but much less than her potential pay with commission. I was also increasing her responsibility with the second location and proposed to pay her less, I wanted more for me which meant that I needed to take from my employee's pay. As you're reading you may be thinking to yourself "what's the problem with that, you were in business to make a profit, what business doesn't want to make more profits? You may be in a similar situation right now, and you are saying to yourself, "I'm a control freak and didn't even know it."

Let's address the "what's wrong with that" believers out there. Yes, I was in business to make a profit, but not at the expense of the staff. As the company grew and expanded the staff roles and responsibilities grew, their pay should have increased as well, not decrease. Honestly, the decrease in pay wasn't about the business being profitable it was about me having more and that's a huge difference. I wanted to shop, travel, and eat more all at the expense of the staff. I was spiraling downward, the baggage was consuming me, and I couldn't see a way out.

For the people thinking to themselves, "I'm a control freak," there is hope. Recovery is possible for you, too. Continue to read my journey. By the end of the book, you will have what you need to create and experience baggage free success.

The "Rainmaker" was aware of her value and contribution to the company, therefore she refused my offer. She decided to work for me, manage the office, and also work for herself at home. The majority of the clients she brought to the company went with her, they were loyal to her, but not the brand. There was a non-compete clause signed, but I wasn't able to compete with the relationship she developed with the clients. I also didn't have authority on the choice of the people. It wasn't that she solicited them, they were connected to her and therefore they found her. I was still spiraling losing and unaware of how the baggage was impacting the business and my personal success.

Control overshadowed my ability to be rational and reasonable. The pain from my grandfather's death, molestation, father's shooting, etc., was the real issue that overshadowed my ability to be reasonable and rational. Control was an effect of the unreleased pain associated with the experiences.

In 2014, I felt like I was in hell's kitchen, I'm not referring to the television show, either. It felt like hell on earth, everything around me seem to be a falling apart. I started the season with the two locations we expanded. I wanted a better quality of staff. I reached out to a temp service that specialized in only placings temps in the accounting industry. I interviewed several applicants and found the perfect one who fit our needs . She had several years of tax and software and management experience per her resume. Tina had a huge personality, her dark curly hair framed her chubby face as she smiled when she spoke the industry language in our first interview. I was impressed with her and the fact that she knew so much about the tax industry. After a second interview, I eventually hired her. Then there was Faith. Faith was a middle-aged, bubbly, outgoing, and upbeat woman with a genuine love for God. I met Faith from within my faith community. She was out of work and needed a job. Since I had the power to hire her, I did just that. We also hired Mandy that year as well. I was working in the office one day when the postal worker came in to deliver the mail. I shuffled through the mail to see what I wanted and what could be thrown away. I saw a handwritten envelope and carefully opened it. I became excited immediately as I recognized it was a resume from Mandy. I received the resume discovering she had years of experience in the industry. I eagerly picked up the office phone and called her and scheduled an appointment. A few days later I was interviewing Mandy, she was a tall slim woman, very reserved and spoke very soft. After interviewing her I hired her, too. This year seemed promising as ever!

After I finished interviewing the new staff, it was time for training. During training, I discovered things about the new employee that I couldn't see during the interview and on their resume. Tina, the applicant with the remarkable experience, who also understood the industry, wasn't as experienced as her resume made her out to be. She struggled with learning how to use and implement the software that she said she had years of experience. . She also had other issues that impaired her ability to perform her duties. I discovered this within one week after hiring her but dismissed it because I had my own agenda. I overlooked the needs of the business due to my need to be in control and appear okay. I allowed her to stay with us and to hurt the business. Allowing her to stay cost more than letting her go and finding a viable replacement for her. She was unproductive and due to her lack of productivity, we lost money.

## PRACTICE WHAT YOU PREACH

There's a lesson that came through this experience: Always do a thorough background check on applicants because a resume is the best version of them on paper. The interview is a presentation of their better self. Also, Checking references allow you to hear other's experience of the person. Social media allows you to see what type of person they present themselves to be via there public persona.

Remember, Faith? The bubbly, outgoing. and upbeat applicant? Well she was difficult to train and didn't take direction well. During training, after being shown the process, and told what to do several times, she would present excuses and justify why it should be done another way so that didn't get to the proper end. Faith and I were having a power struggle, no matter what direction and instruction I presented to Faith. She always had a reason to do something different.

## LESSON LEARNED

Take every application through the hiring process, even if you know them personally. You don't know them as it relates to working with them unless you worked with them previously like myself and the "Rainmaker." If you're having issues with an applicant during training, let them go. There's a saying that says, "Be slow to hire and quick to hire." If it's not working, express that because it will save you more money in the long run.

Mandy, on the other hand, was divinely sent, to me. This is not to say the others were not. Her resume arrived in the mail right when I needed the skills she offered. She interviewed well, went through training quickly; she was a fast learner. Her accounting skills were superb and everything the business needed to get on track she was capable of doing. Although I couldn't articulate or clearly identify the business needs, she had the "It Factor." She was a bookkeeper in every sense of the word. This was an area the business was lacking. Mandy had several years of experience, and she was life to the dying soul of the business. I hired her to be a tax lead but she was sent to help the business clean up its financial mess.

## LET'S GET IT STARTED

When hiring staff, allow them to work in their area of expertise. Never try to get what you want from staff if they have skill sets that would better suit them for another position. They will be more productive when they're working in the area that best fit their skills and you will experience more productive time from them.

As the season progressed, the second location was up and running. The "Rainmaker" left, Tina was revealing more of her true self and abilities, Faith wasn't faithful, and I was spiraling downward. It felt like things were unraveling and I didn't have a hold on anything. Business was really slow because the IRS changed the filing season submission dates which caused employees payroll to be extremely late. Things were falling apart around me, and it was beyond my control and I didn't know what to do. There were days I wanted to hide in hopes it would all go away and I wouldn't have to face anything. Mandy stepped in and rescued the business; however, the tax season was coming to an end, the seasonal employee had been laid off, she and I were the only employee left. She went back over the business bank statements for the previous two years and created a balance sheet, profit and losses statements, and budget for the following year with staff hours, number of staff needed according to business and so much more! Did I mention she was divinely sent to me? It was challenging to go back, review, and collect information, but so worth it to have things organized. I felt a weight lift from me when we did this and I believe things were going to get better. After she completed the books, I took the information and not only applied for a business loan but received it, too. Excited about my accomplishments and feeling in control again, I did as I had always done, I irresponsibly spent the money on myself; clothing, trips, food, you name it. I had yet to release the pain from the baggage that I had and missed true success.

Despite my efforts to stabilize the business with an infusion of cash via the fifteen thousand dollar loan, it was impossible from the place of internal chaos. I, as the CEO, leader, business owner, and boss went, so went the business. I was on a slippery slope, life business, relationships, friends, and family was chaotic, stability from that place felt insurmountable.

I've shared a lot, now let's connect all these experiences to the pain from unreleased baggage. It wasn't the experiences in and of themselves it was the pain connected to the experience that caused the controlling behavior. The pain was the beliefs, thoughts, and feelings that I didn't have the tools to face and process. There's a quote that says "As the leader go so goes the nation." If the leader is wise, understanding, compassionate the people that follow will possess similar characteristics. On the other hand if the leader is rude, disrespectful, or distrusting, the people who follow will possess similar characteristics. If this is true in a larger scale it's also true in a smaller scale. I would like to rephrase it, "As the leader go so goes the company."

The baggage of my past was showing up in my present life and I tried to control it. I tried to manage it, but it wasn't for me to control or manage, I needed to face it, sit with it, speak it, feel it, and process it. Like many CEO's and those at the executive level, I was too busy to deal with my past. I believed because I was the CEO of my company, expanded to two locations, increased the revenue, had a marketing strategy, possessed an American Express gold card with no limit, a high credit score, traveled where I wanted to go, and helped each and every client. I was doing pretty good. The truth is I wasn't okay, the unreleased baggage was impeding upon my ability to sustain, stabilize, and truly succeed in business. I was like many; outwardly successful and in control and inwardly chaotic and out of control. The pain of the unreleased baggage lead the business to bankruptcy.

Yes, in January of 2016, I searched for a bankruptcy attorney. I was desperate and wanted out of the pain and I was willing to go to any lengths for relief.

To be bankrupt is to be insolvent. This means that liabilities exceed assets which causes one to not fulfill repayment obligations to creditors. The external bankruptcy was a reflection of my internal self. I was emotionally bankrupt. The pain from my childhood experiences and unreleased baggage, left me swirling in negative emotions. No matter how hard I tried to be "busy," I couldn't hide from my reality as I went deeper into an emotional bankruptcy and so did the company.

I walked into attorney Sophia's office with my high waist pencil skirt and off white blazer, being the only client in the office I was immediately called back to her office. I sat before her, pulled my white three inch binder from my brown business bag. Everything was organized nice and neat: tax returns, bank statements, all information was in the binder. I looked at her in the eyes, and her whole face appeared to be in shock. She stated with amazement, "You are so organized, I have very few clients that come in with everything together." I confidently replied, "Everything you need is in here." Unbeknownst to her, my presentation of being so organized was a part of the controlling behavior. I was unconsciously controlling how others perceived me, it worked for the untrained eye. She proceeded explained the process and payment details. I pulled out my checkbook and wrote a check for the amount, I wanted out of the pain and this seemed like an out for me so I took it. In March of 2016, the bankruptcy was complete but my life still looked and felt the same. I was still like the "dry drunk" I spoke about earlier.

Confession is good for the soul and I shared my confession about being a control freak with you for you to understand that things aren't always as they appear to be. Someone could have easily judged my behavior not knowing the truth that was underneath the controlling behavior. A truth that I was ashamed to speak of after experiencing it, was a truth that impacted so many people, and a truth that changed my life forever once I confessed it.

If you are reading this book, I'm going to assume you are a in leadership whether it be CEO of a fortune 500 company, small business, organization, or in the executive level of a company. In some capacity you are in leadership and you desire to experience baggage free success. Success that's authentic, accepting, honest, full of integrity and you don't know how. I shared my story that you may know and understand that you are not alone. Your experiences or baggage may not look exactly like mine, but it can lead or has lead you to the same end and it must be released for you to gain true success.

In the next chapters you will discover the proven blueprint for you to release the baggage so you can SURGE into your success.

# CHAPTER 1

## Acknowledge

"No one who achieves success does so without acknowledging the help of others. The wise and confident acknowledge this help with gratitude." ~Alfred North Whitehead

I've confessed I was a control freak and the true cause behind the controlling behavior. I'm turning the corner to offer a guide on how to experience baggage-free success.

In the arena of recovery, even eating disorder recovery, it says the first step to recovery is to acknowledge you have a problem. Here's the truth: no person, angel, or God can help anyone that doesn't have an issue. If you believe you are experiencing true success and everything is going well, there's no issues or unreleased baggage affecting your leadership ability so you should stop reading this book NOW. Go ahead and close the book. Please put it away because it's not for you. You have it all together and I don't want you to spend time trying to improve upon what's good. Could it be possible that you are living where I lived in denial for quite some time before I realized I was a control freak? One of my life spiritual mentors said. " The Nile is more than a river." It's some people's reality. If you didn't get it now, you'll get it later.

I believed denial was like a raft that carried me down a raging river. Imagine being in a river that's moving sixty miles per hour with twist and turns. You're in the river holding onto a brown, thick tree branch that serves as a raft. The branch is all you have to hold onto. You grip the branch tightly as the river waters force you to move down the river. Your upper body is enveloped by the branch as if you were hugging someone you loved. Water splashes in your face, your clothing is soaked due to your submergence into the raging waters. . Your head is above water and the current carries you because you are submerged in the river waters, but your head is above the water. The current carry the river to a drop off and now your floating through the air as the water rushes down to a lake. You land in the lake which is calmer than the raging waters of the river. You're still holding onto the raft, and you didn't make a sound while in the raging waters as your mouth was sealed shut when you landed in the lake.

There are people on the shore beckoning for you to come, but you're still holding on to the raft that you used as your life line in the raging waters. You want to release it but you're afraid, and doubt if you have the emotional and physical capacity to make it to shore. As the people beckon you can hear them, and you're thinking to yourself, "Should I let go or should I continue to hold on? You have a choice to make, what will you choose? This is an example of denial.

Denial served its purpose to get you to a place in life that you didn't have the emotional capacity to journey to until you did. Many like to view denial with a negative lens, but I choose to see it serving a purpose. It's the vehicle that carries you to acknowledgement. Denial helps you get to a place where you can receive the help you need.

The people on shore are there. It is a large crowd of witnesses wanting to help you. These people are employees, friends, family, they all want to help but they can't because you can't hear them calling out to you, reaching out to help you, but their help goes unnoticed because your hand is not extended towards theirs. You have a choice to make. All you only have to do is acknowledge things are unmanageable despite your best efforts to control your life or business because it's somehow spiraled out of control.

I know all too well about this as I've shared in chapter one. I held onto the raft and my drop off point was bankruptcy. I held on until denial carried me to closing the doors of the business, even afterwards, I was still in denial. I was like you floating in the lake, holding on to what use to work. Until I acknowledged my life business and everything within me was unmanageable, I was still in denial. I had to be willing to ask for help, which is extremely difficult for a "control freak", because that somehow meant I wouldn't be in control. It meant I had to risk being vulnerable while sharing my heart, story, pain, feelings, and behavior. This was something I wasn't skilled at doing. I even had to own what I created while in the river of denial.

The first step in this guide is to acknowledge that life is unmanageable and chaotic. If you are reading this, you are already acknowledging your life is unmanageable in some way.

**Question**

1. Where are you? Are you in the raging river or calm lake?
2. Are you ready to acknowledge your life is

unmanageable, if so write below? Ex: *I acknowledged and accept my life is unmanageable right now.*

# Chapter 2

## Believe

**"Beliefs have the power to change reality." ~ Jamella Stroud**

Now that you have acknowledged your business and life has become unmanageable because the unreleased baggage has kept you in denial, continue to imagine with me. You are still in the lake holding on to the tree branch raft, what do you do next? Do you release the raft and swim to shore? Do you call out and ask for help from the crowd of witnesses? What are you to do? Things have settled and the river isn't raging, but you may feel like you are at rock bottom. There isn't a lot going on in the lake. The raging is now happening internally. Honestly the inside raging was always happening, it went unnoticed the external experience overshadowed the your internal reality. While you're in the lake you have time to reflect on how you got to the place you find yourself in.

The next step in the guide causes you to do something internal that will cause an external behavior response. You must believe that a force or powers greater than yourself can turn your business and life around. I call this force and power, God. You get to call your forces of power what works best for you. It's important that you sometimes have a power greater than yourself because as you move through the chapters you will need to rely on this force to support you. If you, like me, struggled with being in control, you also struggled with trusting a force or power greater than yourself. It's okay, you now know that believing and trusting only in yourself does not work because it doesn't support you in releasing the baggage that has impacted your success.

Let's remember the scene, you are in a lake holding onto the tree branch raft, your upper body has enveloped itself around the branch, and you're floating with your head above water in the lake twenty feet from shore. People are around your crowd of witnesses which includes family, friends, employees, strangers all watching and paying attention to you. Some are calling out to you, offering guidance as to how to get ashore. Do you hear them? Can you see them? Do you believe that you deserve to be on shore out of denial, suffering and control? Do you believe you can experience baggage free success? Yes, you believe you deserve to come ashore and return to solid ground, that's why you are reading this book. You know deep down inside that you deserve to release all of the baggage and experience success because you know you deserve to SURGE into success!

The word believe is defined by Google as, "Accept ( something as true) feel sure of the truth of and hold something as on opinion, think or suppose." Therefore the only thing required of you right now is to *accept that someone, something a force and power greater than yourself, I say God, can restore your business and life.* This is simple yet takes effort. There are years upon years of unreleased baggage that has become a part of who you know yourself to be. If you find yourself struggling with this, there must be a willingness to know what's underneath; the unbelief or the inability to accept that you deserve to be baggage free and successful.

Let's look at my story. I had years of pain connected to my childhood experience which resulted in pain in beliefs, thoughts and feeling that supported the controlling behavior amongst other thing. Many of these things I tried to conceal for years, and some of which I believed I overcame while living as a "dry drunk", resurfaced and continued to impact my life. Once I made a choice to believe that I could and deserved to have and experience a baggage free successful life, new and endless possibilities became more and more clear. .

I'm going to assume you are asking yourself the question or wondering to yourself, how do I believe a force greater than myself can and will restore my life and business? How will I know that I believe? Should you just say "I believe"? Should you write something to show you believe? Should you pray? How does this believing thing work? I can only share my experience and my how. I don't believe my way is the only way there are several ways, so please feel free to research and discover the many other ways. On my journey, I discovered this quote "beliefs powers thoughts, thoughts powers feeling, feeling powers behavior." To discover the false beliefs that kept you in denial you must be willing to discover how you feel about your current reality, the thoughts you think about it and behaviors that support your beliefs. I believed I was the best person to do any task in the business, besides those involving technology, which caused me to think my employees were incompetent and they were inadequate. This thought caused me to feel frustrated and then I would micromanage their tasks. If I take this a step further you'll discover there was something under the belief, which was the belief that I didn't deserve to be successful and live without emotional pain. Then there were the belief that "I was not good enough." This belief exposed feelings of inadequacy. I would feel inadequate which caused me to micromanage and attempt to control everything and everybody. Because of the control and micromanaging aspect of my life, I created a toxic work environment. There was no place for a force or power greater than myself in this state, I was the only force that mattered.

I need to know and believe the truth because I still believed that there is a power greater than me who could restore my life and in doing so, I had a chance to experience baggage free success. I knew I believed that God could restore my life and business when I felt differently about my situation. When I was without a dollar in my bank account and efforts to work and find clients, I was still without work. I knew I believed something different in that force and power. It is God who could restore my life and business.

You're in the lake holding onto the raft while your insides are raging. Do you know what you're believing that's cause you to stay stuck and not believe in a greater power outside of yourself? Are you willing to know what you are believing? Let's be clear, returning to solid ground will require your willingness to know what you believe in all parts of your life, and a willingness to allow a power greater than yourself, God, or whomever you believe in, to restore your life.

**Question:**

1. Do you believe a power greater than yourself can restore your life, business, etc.?.
2. Ask your greater power to reveal to you what you believe and the thoughts, feelings, and behaviors connected to it.

# Chapter 3

## Choose

**"The power of choice is the greatest power of humanity." ~ Jamella Stroud**

May of 2018 there was a media frenzy going on about the power of " choice". Kanye West made a statement on TMZ, "When you hear about slavery for four hundred years, four hundred years that sounds like a choice. Like, you were there for four hundred years and it's all ya'll. It's like we're mentally in prison." Personally I don't agree with this thought or idea that slavery was a choice. It would be helpful to define the work choice. According to Dictionary.com the word choice means " An act or instance of choosing, selecting the right, power or opportunity to choose option or something that is preferred or preferable to others; the best part of something. Merriam Webster defines it as " The act of choosing, the act of picking or deciding between two or more possibilities. From these definitions it doesn't sound like there was a lot of choosing going on, but you didn't purchase this book to talk about that, you want to know the next step in the guide to releasing the baggage and gaining success, it's choice!

Although I don't believe slavery was a choice, I do believe having years upon years of the same experiences created a generational trajectory which makes it difficult for someone to choose anything other than what they have previously experienced. Therefore all life choices made are in direct alignment with previous experiences, beliefs, thoughts, and feeling about themselves. Holding onto the baggage in your life is as emotional and mental slavery. The recurring emotional crisis that would cause your life to spiral out of control has a grip on you that can't be released without a choice

In chapter three, you were asked to believe that a power greater than yourself could restore your life and business. We are still imagining you are in the lake holding onto the raft. You're really holding onto your past experiences and the beliefs, thoughts and feeling about them. The raft serves a purpose and you now get to make a choice to surrender your will to the will of your greater power. This can be challenging to say the least especially if you are a control freak because the unreleased baggage came with so many other things, like fear, inferiority, shame, guilt, and anxiety to name a few. The company you run could have been established and operated according to the baggage you brought into it. Your marriage could have been built upon the baggage. The staff you employ could have been hired because of the baggage. Honestly your whole life could be built according to and around the unreleased baggage. Letting go of the raft could mean letting these things go, or letting go the relationship that you have with them. This is a pivotal place in the guide to baggage free success because no one can decide for you. No one can release the raft for you, you have to make a choice to save yourself from yourself.

Unlike every living thing where there are tons of choices to make at this place, there is only one choice, the choose to surrender to your greater power. Sheena Lyengar stated in her TED Talk..... "Choice can develop into the very opposite of everything it represents in America when it is thrust upon those who are insufficiently prepared for it." Choosing to surrender is something you have to be prepared for, If not, you could think you didn't have a choice, and this makes you powerless. If you're powerless, you're a victim and not victorious.

You have a choice to surrender your will to your greater power. Let's define the word, surrender. According to Merriam- Webster the word surrender means, " To give oneself over to something such as influence." Dictionary.com defines it as "To give oneself up, as to some influence, course, emotion. Simply put it's the ability to give your whole self to something. Choosing to surrender would be choosing to resist nothing, and allow things to be as they are, without judgment or criticism of self and the situation.

Choice looks something like the diagram below:

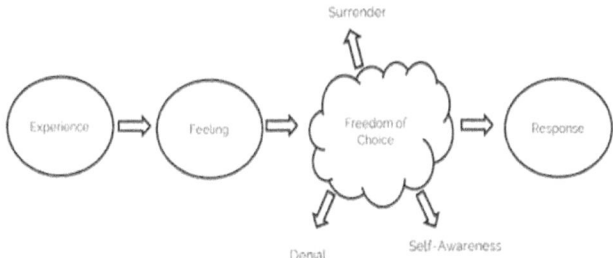

Let's examine one of my life experiences mentioned in the first chapter through the choice framework.

### Experience

At the age of eight I was molested by male and

female family members and it continued with others outside my family as well for a few years. I remained silent about the experience until my twenties.

**Feeling**

Holding this experience in and not speaking about it, I felt worthless, angry, unheard, ashamed, and powerless. I carried those feelings for years not mentioning the experience to anyone until I couldn't be silent anymore, because I had a choice to make.

**Choice**

The first choice I made, although unconscious, was denial. I tried to live my life as if I wasn't impacted by the experience. It was if I erased it from my memory, but it wasn't erased from my emotions. Denial is a choice and it's one that serves a purpose until it doesn't anymore. Once I was ready to deal with the truth of the experience I chose to become self-aware. Willing to allow the pain of the feeling to resurface feeling the full impact of all the emotional anger, worthlessness, shame etc. I choose to confront these feelings relating to the experience. From the place of self- awareness I could choose to surrender my will over to my greater power,

God.

You are in the lake, and you have moved from the denial raging river to a place of self-awareness. The journey to solid ground is via the swim of choosing to surrender.

## Question

1. Are you willing to make a choice to surrender your life and will over to your greater power, God, as you understand? Be honest. It's okay if you're not there yet?

If you are truly ready say this prayer out loud and write it down:

"God, I offer myself to Thee—to build with me and to do with me as Thou wilt Relieve me of the bondage of self, that I may better do Thy will. Take away my difficulties, that victory over them may bear witness to those I would help of Thy Power, Thy Love, and Thy Way of life. May I do Thy will always!" Alcoholics Anonymous. (2001) New York, NY: AA World Services, Inc., 63.

## Alternatively to Pray

I, [state your name], am now willing to commit myself to serving the greater good and be of cheerful service to those around me. I am willing to make my service to a higher purpose more important than any desire for recognition or reward. When filled with fear and self-doubt, as I am sure to be at times, I resolve to remember my willingness and do the next right thing that prepares me to be of better service. I gratefully embrace this opportunity to turn my will and my life over to serve a useful purpose. *Eating Disorders Anonymous The Story of How We Recovered from Our Eating Disorders (2016) by the General Service Board of Eating Disorders Anonymous, Inc.*

*Surrender Phase*

# CHAPTER 4

# Inventory

**"Looking within for the answer to the problem is what great leaders do." Jamella Stroud**

" A business which takes no regular inventory usually goes broke. Taking commercial inventory is a fact finding and fact facing process. It is an effort to discover the truth about the stock in the company. One objective is to disclose damaged or unsellable goods, and to get rid of them promptly and without regret." 12stepsprogram.com

Inventory is about you. Your ability to see what's within you that has caused you to be where you are. A question I normally ask myself for inventory's sake is, "How did I get here?. As stated above, inventory is a fact finding and fact facing process. It's a quest to discover the truth about who you really are versus who you show up as. Who you are is your character, which is formed by age seven and is comprised of your beliefs, thoughts and feelings. These beliefs, thoughts, and feelings drive your behavior and they're connected to your life experiences.

In the recovery circle, this is called a fearless, moral inventory. I must say first hand that it requires you to be fearless because it will challenge you to see something about yourself that you have been unwilling or able to see. It will cause you to think something you were unable or willing to think. It will cause you to feel something you were unable or willing to feel. If I'm honest, if it were possible to avoid this step, I would. The years I spent binging and purging as a bulimic and the years of being a control freak were unconscious attempts to avoid this step. Once I surrendered to the process and my greater power, God, there was no more avoiding, numbing, or hiding, I had to face myself. I had to take inventory to understand and experience totally restoration.

I want to go into in depth details of my struggle with bulimia, but I did in my book *Bulimic To Believer*. The entire book is an example of a fearless moral inventory. I was willing to go into unchartered places within myself to understand, face and forgive myself. This part of the guide to baggage free success takes courage and bravery as it is not for the faint of heart.

Unless you've been living under a rock, I take it that you've seen the movie, *Titanic*. This was about a huge cruise ship that was built by engineers and architects who believed the amazing ship couldn't sink, but later discovered the ship could and would in fact sink.

Imagine a huge ocean liner one hundreds thirty three feet long sinking in the middle of the Pacific Ocean and touches the bottom of the ocean floor. The ocean floor is about 36,200 feet deep, you're saying to yourself. That's really deep. The deepest part of the ocean is called, the challenger deep. Now think about the Titanic being excavated from the depths of the ocean, it's would take a lot of energy and effort, plus people power to accomplish this.

The ocean represents the subconscious part of the brain. During inventory the goal is to bring what's in the subconscious to consciousness. This is the process of fact finding and fact facing, and it requires time, support, courage and effort. Following the guide of the first three steps prepares you to take inventory. Like the Titanic that lives in the deepest parts, there is something that lives within the depths of your subconscious mind, and taking inventory provides an opportunity to discover those hidden or suppressed beliefs, thoughts, and feelings. Your time is now!

You're still in the lake holding onto your tree branch raft that has been your safety net. You are safe; however, you desire to be on shore. The question is, are you willing to go through the fact finding and fact facing process to discover the truth about who you are? How you lead, how you interact with your employees, family and friends have a greater impact on your experiences, and the resentment you hold within, that support you holding on.

Before you decide if you are ready to take courageous inventory, allow me to share with you the things I discovered about myself and how it impacted the people I lead. While taking inventory, I discovered I had a deep rooted feeling of unworthiness. Those feelings stemmed from me being labeled as "bad" during childhood. were deep feeling In elementary school, I was in trouble for "talking too much", and I was labeled as "bad" for it. Later in middle and early part of high school, I fought and was called "bad" for this behavior as well. When I had done something they didn't like, I was restricted access to things that the "good girls" had access to. Due to me being labeled "bad", I believed I was undeserving of true success like the "good girls".

Having that one thing impacted my ability to lead my staff. That deep rooted feeling caused me to project the same feelings onto them. I found it difficult to truly appreciate them and have compassion for their mistakes. I even struggled with a pay increase for them due to the belief and feelings of unworthiness.. It was in the depths of my subconscious and it took hard work to excavate the beliefs, thoughts and feelings.

I also discovered fear in my inventory. I found fear of all kinds, fear of failure, success, other people's opinion of me, fear of rejection, and fear of my imperfection. I was told I was a "bad girl" in my childhood, so I strived to do good and be a "good girl". As the CEO of my first company, J'S Tax Service, I mastered the mask of perfection. I believed if I wasn't perfect, I was bad, and if I was bad, then I wouldn't achieve my goals, If didn't achieve my goals, I was a failure. *(This is the cycle of dysfunctional thinking)* Holding onto the fear caused me to micromanage the employees in an attempt and effort to look perfect. I was unwilling to ask for help to develop the business because I believed if I needed help, that would make me imperfect and therefore expose me for not knowing what I didn't know which would have made me appear stupid. All of these thoughts were in my beliefs, thoughts, and feelings inventory, which wasn't conscious because they were in my subconscious lying dormant.

Having fear in my inventory wreaked havoc and damaged in my ability to lead. In my quest to maintain perfection and look perfect, I was causing and creating more problems for myself and the employees, The atmosphere in my company wasn't pleasant as long as I was there.

Now that you are familiar with things in my inventory, are you ready to discover what's in your beliefs, thoughts and feelings inventory? Do you know how it has impacted your relationships? Unlike the other guides, this part of the process requires you to fully engage.

**Question**

**Identify where you are by answering the following questions.**

1. What are you angry about? ( Be sure to consider every area and aspect of your life.) Write whatever comes to mind) Ex: I am angry because I lost my business

2. Identify the challenge. ( What has the anger prevented you from doing/being). EX: The anger prevents me from taking the adequate steps to develop a business again.
3. Identify the People. ( Who are you angry with?) EX: I am angry with God.
4. Identify Truth. (Use emotional chart at the back of book and identify what's under the anger.) EX: The feeling beneath the anger with God is fear and shame,
5. Speak what's on your mind. (Vent or write what you really want to say, it doesn't have to be nice). EX: The anger would speak to God and say: "You left me when I needed you most during the downward spiral of the business. You abandoned me, I hate you right now for that."
6. Speak what is on your heart (Share heart, softer feelings of vulnerability). Pretend you are five to seven years old. What else do you want the specific person to know? EX: I want God to know that I'm afraid of going into business again because it hurt so bad to lose everything.
7. Ask for what you want. ( Your adult self speaks here). What are you asking for

from the specific person/people with whom you are angry? I am asking God to give me the courage and strength to start again without fear of the outcome.

8. Forgive Yourself. ( Forgiveness is the ticket to freedom). Reflect on everything you've discovered and ask yourself if you are willing to let yourself off the hook). What are you willing to forgive yourself for /about? EX: I'm willing to forgive myself for blaming God for the closing of the business

9. Sometimes you are not ready to forgive and it's okay, Just be aware. Is there anything you are not willing to forgive yourself for /about. EX: I am not willing to forgive myself for _____.

10. Forgive Someone Else. (The people you hold resentment towards are human like you and make mistakes. What are you willing to forgive people for? EX: I am willing to forgive God for not showing up the way I thought God should on my behalf.

11. Sometimes you're simply not ready to forgive another person and it's okay, just be aware. Is there anyone you are not willing to forgive? EX: I am not willing to

forgive \_\_\_\_\_ because \_\_\_\_\_

It's important that you share this with someone. Someone you trust that will allow you to be honest and they will be objective to support and hold you accountable.

# Chapter 5

## Admit

**"Admitting doesn't make you bad or wrong, it makes you courageous. Only the brave will admit they are flawed." ~Jamella Stroud**

According to Google, the word, admit, has two definitions. One definition states, "to confess to be true or be the case." The second definition states, "to allow someone to enter a place." Both definitions are equally important in the guide to baggage free success. When a person admits something about themselves, beliefs, thoughts, feelings or any other behavior, its normally something they have hidden about themselves, whether done consciously or at the subconscious level. When something is hidden at the level of subconscious, it's about who we really are. It's not something that can be easily seen about on their own. Others may be experiencing, or have experienced the behavior of the hidden thing and the person could be unaware of the impact their behavior has on others. It's important the other guiding steps are completed before this one. In chapter five you had the opportunity to excavate and explore your beliefs, thoughts, feelings and behaviors that were in your subconscious and the need to be brought to the level of consciousness to be shared with someone you trust for accountability purposes.

I'm not big on organized religion, but I must say Catholics have mastered the art of admitting, or as the definition says confessing. For years, they have understood the gift of confession and the liberating power of it.

When you admit your flaws, it allows others to enter into that place with you, that hidden, secret, sacred place. When you allow others into your hidden, secret, and sacred places you are allowing your greater power to enter that place, that hidden place you wanted to hide and conceal from the world. One of my favorite sayings I repeat often to myself and my daughter is " In time all things will be revealed, there is no hidden thing that won't be recovered and secret thing that won't be revealed." You can make a choice to reveal things about yourself or through life they will be revealed. When you choose to admit something about yourself, it reduces its power over you. I've vowed to tell my own story in this lifetime. No one will have the opportunity to tell my story because I'll share it myself. I choose to admit I was a control freak.

Admitting your flaws and faults is something that should be done in a safe, comfortable space with someone you trust that can provide feedback or ask thoughts provoking questions to further support you in uncovering whatever is hidden. It wouldn't be wise to admit something about yourself on social media that you haven't fully processed and shared in a safe place with others. It took quite some time before I was ready to admit I was a control freak. I lived in the denial where I justified my behavior which kept me stuck. I was willing but I wasn't ready to admit. In my distorted thinking, to admit meant I was wrong; not my behavior but my being. The reality is to admit meant I had to be responsible for my experiences and actions. I had to see myself for who I was at the lowest and highest thinking. I didn't have an issue with seeing the great and wondering things about myself, it was the lowest thinking and feeling I struggled with that caused my inner vision to be impaired. To keep from looking at myself I would say things like "I just like things to be done a certain way and it should done the way I want it done, I'm just picky." An employee once said to me, "I feel micromanaged when you tell me how to do what I know to do, and that's a form of control." The truth was that I was controlling and it had very little to do with my employer.

Admitting is surrendering the need to be right and the need to control others by falsifying self through controlling behavior. This is the most freeing experience you will ever have afterwards. It's like going skydiving. You enter an airplane with other trained, licensed skydivers who explain the process as the plane ascends into the sky. The guide puts the equipment on himself before he walks you through the process of putting your equipment on. There are others in the plane for support to make sure the diver and you have what you need before the dive. Next, It's time to jump. Your heart is racing, throat tightens, and stomach turns as you're being strapped to the professional diver. You look out the door unable to see the ground. You said, yes, and now it's beyond your control from this point. One, two... out the door you go descending to earth 120 miles per hour for a few seconds. You began to scream because it's exhilarating, then the parachute opens and descends at 17 miles per hours. You see things you've never seen before, you feel something you never felt before. You've lost control and gained freedom in the moment. You're approaching the ground, it's time to land, and you're still pumped from the explosion. You survived! You made it to solid ground safely, everything intact, and still connected to the professional. The professional skydiver was not negatively impacted by your internal experience at all. When you disconnect from the professional, you are filled with joy and gratitude for your experience and his craft. You realize he does what he does so you can experience bliss, joy, freedom, and adventure. You're ready to do it again because you loved the feeling. That's how admitting your fault and flaws feel. It feels scary in the beginning but as you continue to share the first time, you began to feel the freedom and you experience bliss because you were willing to lose control and allow yourself to fall into truth and freedom.

You're in the lake holding onto your tree branch raft, it's safe, comfortable and familiar. You have a choice, what will you choose, freedom or continue with control. You're reading this book, and you've made it this far therefore I'm going to assume you're choosing freedom via admitting your flaws. The more you admit to your greater power and other humans the closer you get to freedom. The more you lose control the more of your life and business is restored.

## Question

1. Who are you going to admit your flaws to? ( This can be one person or a small group. Make sure these are people you trust wholeheartedly.)
2. When will you admit your flaws? Set a date and time to keep you accountable to yourself. Remain flexible because you don't want to control the process.

# Chapter 6

## Willing & Ready

**"Being willing does not mean being ready, but you must learn to be both to experience success." ~Jamella Stroud**

It was recently that I discovered the difference between being willing and ready. I've used the words differently in sentences but wasn't quite sure of the distinct difference between the two. I'm one who has always thought of myself as being willing. willing to try new things, willing to explore, willing to push myself beyond the ceiling, I believed I was willing, but not as ready as I would have liked to believe I was. There's a difference between these words that we must explore that will support you in releasing the baggage and claim success.

According to Google, Willing means, "eager or prepared to do something." I would define willingness as the ability to accept the changes in life, business and adjust accordingly quickly.

After reading the book, "*Who Moved My Cheese by Spencer Johnson. MD.*I realized I wasn't as willing as I thought. Honestly on a scale of one to ten, one being less willing and ten being most willing, I would have ranked at two. Knowing and admitting this truth about myself was eye opening and refreshing. I know longer had a need to deceive myself into believing something about myself that I wanted to be true. I could allow the truth to be as it was. I was like the character, Hem, in the book, and my goal in life is to be like Sniff, truth is at the time I write, I'm not there yet, but I'm embracing, Haw, another character, by being open to the exploration. To know more about these characters you'll have to read the book. I'm not going to spoil it for you.

Your level of willingness is directly impacted by your level of acceptance. The larger your circle of acceptance, the more willing you are. The smaller your circle of acceptance, the less willing you are. What's not accepted can't be removed, and for character flaws to be removed, one has to be revealed; however, it can only be revealed when you are willing to first see it, accept it, then be ready to remove it.

Willingness is so much of a process that it took

me five years to be willing to realize I was unwilling, stubborn, and totally resistant to the change that was happening in my life. I was moving externally but not going anywhere because I was the in the same place internally. Imagine a hamster on a wheel, it's moving expending energy to only be in the same place when the movement stops.

Now imagine you're still in the lake holding onto the tree branch raft just floating in the water. Now is the time to make a choice. A choice to not only be willing, but willing to accept and realize you are still in the same place because of your own resistance, stubbornness, control and other character flaws that you've discovered in chapter five. Are you willing to allow your greater power to remove your character defects? You may be thinking, how is your greater power (God) going to remove a character defect? The answer is simple. If you could have removed them by now, they would have been gone by now, and you would be further along than you are right now. You couldn't and can't so someone such as your greater power that's deep within and works inside and outside of you has to intervene, but you must be willing. If you're unwilling or would be a violation and assault to your person and your greater power, God for me, isn't in the business of causing you harm.

Now let's talk about readiness. Willingness is the ability to accept the changes in life or business and adjust accordingly and quickly.

Being ready is different. Google defines ready as, "Prepared (someone or something for an activity or purpose." I decided to dig deeper, so I searched "YouTube University' for the best video that explained what "being ready" really meant. I found a TedX Talk entitled "Be Ready" by Sarah Horn. Sarah Horn is a voice and music teacher who had an opportunity of a lifetime presented to her at the Hollywood Bowl where she was able to grace the stage with one of her favorite singers, Kristin Chenoweth. A video of Sarah and Kristin went viral on a YouTube and by overnight, she was all over YouTube and other social platforms. This happened because Sarah was ready. While at the concert, Kristin randomly choose an audience member to come on stage to sing with her. Unbeknownst to her, she choose a voice teacher who had practice for years, studied the craft, rehearsed the specific song over and over for no other reason than to be better than she was the day before. Sarah didn't have a clue she'll be called forth from the audience. She wasn't able to control the show because she was a participant like everyone else and when chosen, she came forth. Little did the crowd know she was ready in that moment. If at any point in her journey she felt shy or inadequate, those defects were removed in the moment she accepted the invitation to come forth from the crowd

In Sarah's TedX Talk, she asked, "Was everyone shocked that a voice teacher could sing? I think everyone was shocked that a random girl came out of nowhere and was ready."

Being ready requires work and preparation. I was in denial for quite some time. I believed I needed to say I was ready to be ready. I was unaware of the work and effort that went into being ready. The years of training, the level of devotion, and the discipline required to be ready is work. To surge into success you have to embrace the process. The previous guiding steps are a must for readiness and preparation. They work There's a saying "Old habits die hard." I believe this is so true. If you have attempted to control your life all of your life, be gentle with yourself because surrendering will not be automatic or your natural response. Control may be your go to place when things feel chaotic for you or you're not sure how the end will be. If control is your first response, surrendering is going to take work, effort, time, practice, honesty, grace and forgiveness. It's possible to be willing but not ready. Willingness is the catalyst for being ready. You can't be ready without first being willing.

Sarah's video went viral because she was ready. What the video didn't show were all the training and practice she went through for that moment. There's a Bible verse that says, "Count it all joy"........... I'm sure in that moment on stage with her musical "idol," Sarah was able to count it all joy, the long practices, nights of studying, and years of school were all worth it for that moment. Your moment is coming. The moment for you to release control and make a conscious choice to emerge from the denial. You have been holding onto the raft for too long and you have done the work to be ready to leave the lake. Are you ready?

## Question

1. Have you made and honest effort to this point?
2. Are you ready for your greater power to remove the defects of your character. Be honest. If not, say so?

*Release Phase*

# CHAPTER 7

## Ask

**"Asking for what you need or want is powerful, it opens doors for you to receive."
Jamella Stroud**

Now that you are willing and ready to release control to surge into success, you are ready to take another huge step. Ask your greater power, God, to remove them for you.

If you could remove your defects, such as control, by yourself, you would have done so by now. You in and of yourself couldn't, so you need help to do so. To receive help, you must ask for help. Asking for help for a control freak, like myself, requires humility and vulnerability. You must know and express you don't have it all together. You have to own all the character flaws that were companions of being a control freak, and I know there are several companions.

Remember my story in chapter one, *Confessions of a Control Freak?* I was a control freak in business and life. I wanted everything to go my way and it was all about what was best for me. I didn't trust my employees to do what they were hired to do. I was greedy because I wanted more money for myself at the expense of my employees. I lived in denial about the state of the business, because I watched it go downhill. I lied to myself and my employees about what was happening with the business, because I was ashamed and prideful. Self-centeredness consumed me in my head; it was my business, my clients, my money, my, my, my. I didn't share the ownership of the company with the employees. I didn't involve them in the vision or allow them to have a voice about the direction we were going. They were valuable assets and would have provided amazing ideas, but I didn't create a space that was conducive for them to thrive.

I understand it feels safe and comfortable to keep your flaws. You're not sure what life would look like apart from it. How would you be if you weren't a control freak? How would people perceive you without it? Will you be an effective leader without it? There are a lot of questions that can pop up in your head, I get it so allow me to continue to paint a picture. Continue to imagine with me; don't resist, allow yourself to imagine.

You're in the lake holding onto your tree branch raft, going nowhere yet holding on. You're willing and ready to come ashore where people are waiting to celebrate you. People want to help you but they can't without your permission, because they love and respect you and your choice, they wait for you to ask for help. You hold on tight to your raft, take a deep breath inhale in and exhale out. You open your mouth and began to yell, "Help me please, someone help me, I've been here for too long. Will someone please help me out!" You're yelling, kicking creating a huge commotion, but the raft begins to drift closer and closer to shore, and before you know it, you're at the shoreline. Someone you admire, who loves you unconditionally, extends their right hand to you. You look up because you are stunned that you are close enough to receive help. Your eyes meet their eyes and you see light radiate from within. You slowly extend your right hand until you interlock with theirs. People are watching. There is a crowd of witnesses that have gathered and waiting for you to join them. They're cheering for you, chanting, "You can do it, yes you can!" The person holding your hand places their left hand on top of your right hand, now both of their hands are on top of your right hand. Both hands are stretched out to you. They say to you, just look at me, focus on me, watch me, stay connected with me. Your eyes focused and ears listening you do just that. They tell you to ask what you need help with, what are the character flaws you want removed. You open your mouth and began to speak each one. As you speak them you are being lifted from the lake. When you say the last one, you realize you are back on shore. You're no longer in isolation and alone left to yourself to figure it out. The person looking you in your eyes say to you, "You did great work, I didn't pull you but I simply held your hand and you climbed up by yourself. Every time you asked for a flaw to be removed you came up a little higher". In amazement you began to celebrate yourself because you were able to ask humbly for help and received the help you needed.

Because you are ready to humbly ask your greater power, God, to remove your character flaws repeat this prayer below. Use the list from chapter five

**Prayer**
"My Creator, God, Father, Lord, I am now willing

to surrender all of me the bad, good, ugly and great. I ask that you now remove from me every single flaw and defect of character in belief, thought, feeling and behavior _____(speak them) that stand in the way of my total usefulness to you and my fellow sisters and brothers in the earth. Grant me strength, as I go out from here to fulfill my purpose in life. I ask, allow, believe it's possible, Amen.

**Question**

1. You lost control, how does it feel?
2. You celebrated yourself how does that feel?

# Chapter 8

## Willing to Amend

*"Sometimes being willing is the only requirement. Are you willing? " Jamella Stroud*

You have done some amazing work so far. Your true success is before you at this point in your journey, and there's still work to do.

Because you are reading this book and you've made it this far, I believe you are a part of an amazing group of people within the earth who are willing to go to any length for themselves because they know it's worth it for their soul.

This part if the journey requires you to take action. You are asked to make a list of all persons harmed by your behavior. A list should be created from chapter five when you performed inventory. If there are people you need to add that didn't come up initially, add them. This harm could have been done to staff, family, friends or anyone that was harmed by your behavior. At this point there's nothing to do only to be willing to make amends.

Let's define the difference between hurt and harm. Dr. Cloud in the book, *Boundaries,* make a great distinction between the two stating: "There's a huge difference between hurt and harm. We all hurt sometimes in facing hard truths, but it makes us grow. It can be the source of huge growth. Harm is when you damage someone. Facing reality is usually not a damaging experience even though it can hurt."

Let's say you go to the dentist for your normal routine cleaning. As the hygienist cleans your teeth, she discovers you have a cavity and need a root canal to save the tooth. You agree with the procedure and move forward with scheduling. On your next visit, the root canal is performed. The dentist sticks a needle in the gum for numbing purposes/anesthesia for the procedure. Upon completion after the medication wears off, your mouth starts to hurt, luckily you were prescribed some pain medication for it. In this situation you experienced a level of hurt. The dentist work caused hurt, discomfort and pain, but it was for your best interest. If you didn't get the root canal, you could have experienced a harm resulting in improper care of your tooth.

Although there was hurt involved, you returned to your dentist the next time and continued your relationship with him/her. As Dr. Cloud stated, "We all hurt sometimes when facing truth."

Harm is different, let's take the same situation and add a twist. This time as the dentist performs the root canal he/she drills too deep into your tooth hitting the gum which causes excessive bleeding. The root canal was halted and couldn't be completed that day due to the bleeding and swelling of the gum line. You were sent home and asked to return the next day to complete the procedure. You left with so much excruciating pain, all you could do was lay on your couch in the fetal position. During the night, infection set in, and the next day you returned to the dentist office only to find out you would need surgery to remove the tooth do to the infection. You're devastated because you trusted this dentist. You move forward with the surgery, but later sued the dentist office for negligence due to the harm you experienced. You changed dentists and never return to that office again. Due to your experience, you now have reservations about dentists. In this situation, you were harmed.

Harm in relationships causes people to decline or diminish performance, withdrawal from the relationship, and seek justice. If someone you are close with blocks your phone call, block you on social media, withdraw in your presence, does not respond to you, it's a possibility they feel harmed.

- Personal decline- If you have an employee that starts with your company coming to work bright and energetic then over time their demeanor changes, their dressing style change. In your presence they withdraw, it could be they have experienced a harm.

- Finished performance- If an employee was once very productive, completed task in a timely manner, self-motivated, and over time you noticed they appear unfocused, unproductive, and a loss of creativity, chances are they could have been harmed.

Hurt causes pain but the relationship can be maintained. Harm causes pain and disconnection from the relationship. Take a moment and reflect on your life now that you are clear on the difference between hurt and harm and think about people in your work environment, family, friends, relationships you have caused harm. Be willing to make amends by creating a list of the person, actions behaviors or characteristics that caused the harm.

The "rainmaker" from chapter one came to the business the second year. She was energetic, determined, excited and a team player for the business. She brought in new clients and generated a lot of business. I started her off with a hourly pay and commission, and each season she had a pay increase. In year four, I became greedy and wanted more money for myself and proposed a pay cut to her that was significantly lower. I proposed to remove her commission and increase her hourly pay. She refused the offer and choose to leave the business. My actions caused a financial harm to her. The greed caused me to inflict harm upon her and her family financially. It was not my intention to cause harm, but I did. Harm can be caused intentionally or unintentionally, therefore your intention doesn't make a difference in the person's feelings.

Years later after realizing the nature of my wrongs, I went to her and made amends. I realized the impact of my harm towards her and I was sorrowful that I harmed her. Remember, this isn't a reason for you to sit in self-pity or beat yourself up about what you have done. It's for you to be very honest with yourself and be willing to go back to the person and admit it.

You have made your way out the lake now you are surrounded by the crowd of witnesses that were cheering you on the whole time. Look around at who's there. You may find that some of the people who were there aren't due to the harm and experience. You may find some people are still there, although they may have experienced harm. All that's asked of you here is to be willing to make amends and your willingness in your ability to write the list. If you don't feel willing to make an amends because someone has done something to you, I suggest as in AA and EA that you pray for the wellbeing of that person, success, and health until you find the courage to be willing.

## Question

If you are not willing to make amends with someone who harmed you and you harmed them, pray for them using this prayer daily until you find the courage.

God, Creator, Universal, Higher power I pray for _____ I wish him/her peace, joy and love in all of his/her life. I recognize and honor your spirit within _____, he/she is a reflection of the divine and radiates light in the earth.

Allow his/her light to continuously shine.

If you are ready to make amends use your list from chapter five add anyone that came up that's not on your list: Remember you are only taking responsibility for what you have done, don't own anything more.

| Names | Harm Caused |
|---|---|
| Examples: Lisa Hill | Example: I was greedy and my greed impacted her financially. I underpaid and overworked her. |

# Chapter 9

## Amends

**"It takes humility to go back and apologize to someone you've harmed; however, the peace that comes with it is unexplainable." ~Jamella Stroud**

You have done amazing work to this point. You should celebrate yourself, because this isn't for the faint of heart.

In this chapter you are going to step it up a notch. You are asked to reach out to the people you've harmed by your controlling behavior and baggage you held onto. Remember when you were in the lake floating on the tree branch raft unwilling to clearly see yourself and unwilling to do something, different people where being harmed by your inaction. I defined harm in chapter eight, if your behavior caused people, employees, and friends to leave chances as they were harmed. Imagine you're still on the shore of the lake. Look around and see who's still there.

Is everyone still in attendance as you floated aimlessly down the river of denial.? Are the same people there while you sat in the lake? There are people who left, some left for others reason and some left because they were harmed.

Making amends is going to require you to get up and take action to reach out as this requires great courage, vulnerability, transparency, honesty, and willingness to experience feeling rejected. Not everyone that you reach out to make amends will be open and willing to receive them, that's a part of the process. You will need counsel and support during this process, because it can feel painful and uncomfortable to step outside and be accountable for your actions and own how they impact others. This is a process not a sprint, allow your greater power to lead you as you enter this part of the process.

I know firsthand how this experience can go. During my journey of making amends I reached out to a dear friend. I realized I harmed her by providing unsolicited feedback about her business and the trajectory in which it was going. She was offended and harmed by my feedback causing her to withdraw from the friendship. Before you think to yourself that's not a harm, it was a harm for her. What harms one person is different from what could harm another. I didn't pursue her or have contact with her for over a year and half. I sought guidance and support before reaching out so I wouldn't abandon the process if things didn't go as I hoped. I reached out via text asking if and when would be available to talk so that I may make amends for the harm I caused and repair our relationship. She replied, "I understand your reasoning for contacting me and appreciate your thoughts, but I have moved on with my life. You have not caused me any harm. I have forgiven you and want to move forward with my life. Can we agree to move forward without having any contact with one another." I was heartbroken and saddened by the response because I would have liked to have her as a friend again, but that's not what she wanted, so I honored and respected her choice. I responded by saying, "I honor and respect your wishes." I expressed my feelings of the experience with my support system and allowed myself to feel sad. After that experience I felt rejected and didn't want to reach out to another person because I didn't want to experience that again.

When preparing to make amends, it not important to share your new insight or revelation about what you've learned. Your purpose and goal is to be brief and explain what you desire to do and why. State what you did, apologize for that belief, thought, feelings, words or behaviors. Don't make mention or reference what the other person did because it's not about them it's about you. Ask for forgiveness from the person, but don't have an expectation of the person and their response, or about how you yourself will respond to the process.

It's important to understand you must be willing to go to any length to set right the wrongs towards others in belief, thought, feeling, words and behaviors. Having support like a trusted, objective coach, counselor, advisor is essential to this process of making amends. If making an amend would further harm you or the other person, it's important that you don't. In situations where someone could experience harm, you would make a life amend, meaning the area of harm that was inflicted upon the other person you become aware of and live your life apart from the behavior and donated time or talent to give back in that area. If the harm would be inflicted upon yourself, likewise you wouldn't address the person.

Let's say you were in an emotionally abusive relationship and the person was also manipulative. Whenever you communicated with that individual, you were the one with a problem and they didn't take responsibility for their action. You would be the one who would appear crazy in front of others as that person belittled you. As a response you would yell and scream at them, call them names, etc. This example may be a situation that could cause you further harm by attempting to make amends, therefore you acknowledge your behavior and become aware and change your response to that type of behavior. You could also write a letter to the person and not send it, if you feel like you need to say what you need to say, or you could role play with your coach, counselor or advisor.

There are times when financial amends need to be made; however, be sure when making these amends that your family isn't deprived from their needs. You must put a plan in place to repair the debt or debts in full no matter how slow as long as you are consistent.

Once you begin to make amends when you are halfway through your list, you will begin to experience something different in your life. Your life will began to take shape and your new experience will be likened to the ninth step, "Promise" in alcoholic anonymous:

"If this phase becomes painstaking in our development, we will know a new freedom and a new happiness. We will not regret the past nor wish to shut the door on it. We will comprehend the word serenity and we will know peace. No matter how far down we have fallen, we will see how our experiences can benefit others. The feeling of uselessness and self-pity will disappear. We will lose interest in selfish things and gain interest in our fellows. Self-seeking will slip away. Our whole attitude and outlook upon life will change. Fear of people and economic insecurity will leave us. We will intuitively know how to handle situations which use to baffle us. We will see that our service to God, our Higher Power, or the greater good, has done for us what we could not do for ourselves. Are these extravagant promises? We think not. They are being fulfilled among us - sometimes quickly, sometimes slowly. They will always materialize if we work for them." (Alcoholics Anonymous (2001) New York, NY: AA World Service, Inc., 83-84.

## Question

1. What feeling came up for you as you moved in making amends?
2. Did you find it difficult to make amends?

*Maintenance Phase*

# CHAPTER 10

# Continue

"Until self-searching becomes a regular habit, you want advance much in life." ~ Unknown

You are now ready for a new way of living and leading. You have done a great work with the first nine guiding steps to baggage free success. The guides are foundational principles on which you will build upon the rest of your life. As promised in step nine, you will know a new freedom and life will make sense. Every experience will connect to each other.

It's imperative that you continue to be self-aware and conscious of your beliefs, thoughts, feelings, and behaviors and admit when you are wrong promptly. From this point you will find it easier to be self- aware and admit your faults. Daily you should be aware of your intentions and motivation, asking yourself are you taking care of your basic needs, spiritually, emotionally, and physically. Are you connected to other people around you? Are you of service to others? Stepping into success from this place depends on your ability to be self-aware, emotionally intelligent, and your support system, and all things you have cultivated through this process. At this point you should have support built into your life, places to go, or people to talk to when your life begins to feel unmanageable. You should also have tools in place to support you such as journaling, art therapy, etc.

I personally live this reality. I began journaling in 2015 on a daily basis and it has transformed my life! I reflect on my day, my beliefs, thoughts, feelings, and behaviors, I even look back at previous years to see if I've moved or if I'm having similar issues. You will be surprised how this has really changed my life. I'm also participating in Eating Disorders Anonymous, a celebrate recovery group that meets weekly, and a business support group that meets monthly. I built these support systems into my life and began to take the steps toward continuing daily inventory. As life evolves, the nature of your support group and the type of group may change, but it's imperative you have infused support, reflection, and intention into your life for you to experience baggage free success.

When the day is done, take a few minutes to sit and reflect on your day. Make a note to talk about the things that transpired throughout the day as this is a part of the continuation to be self-aware and conscious of yourself and actions. For this guiding step to be fulfilled in your life, you must live in the presence. There are times when the past will show up in your present and it's up to you to be aware of what's happening so that you may respond differently than before. If you are not present, it's going to be difficult for you to recognize your past is showing up in your present.

Personal inventory in chapter five is all about self-awareness, and self-awareness is about truth. Being aware of your truth in belief, thought, feeling, and behavior is your way to success and the way you will continue to experience success.

Let's continue to image you are on the shore, making it out of denial, you did the work to make it back into society with others, connecting and reconnecting with people who will support you on your journey and life of success without baggage. There are some people from your past that are a part of your present life because they were willing to forgive your behavior towards them. There are some people who are not because they were not willing to make amends and that's okay. You have done your part in re-establishing relationships. From this place you know and believe you can experience baggage free success as your authentic self. You are leaving the side of the river and lake because you now know and value the tools you have picked up during your process. You honor and value the people and relationships that are in your life. Not only do you promptly admit when you are wrong you also are now able to share your true feeling with others regarding their behavior and how it impacts your life.

Remember the quote from chapter five, "A business which takes no regular inventory usually goes broke." Taking regular inventory is a fact finding and fact facing process. It's an effort to discover the truth about the stock in the company. One objective is, "To discover damaged or unusable goods to get rid of them promptly and without regret." When daily inventory is taken, it helps you discover the truth sooner than later and discard whatever within that's not helpful to your growth, development, and whatever will hinder you from true success.

As you can see this part of the process is all about maintenance. As it would be irresponsible to purchase a new car and never change the oil and expect it to continue without having problems, it's as equally irresponsible to not continue to have daily inventory checkups to see where you are as it relates to where you would like to be.

There are several practices you can put in place to support you on your journey such as:

- Gratitude Journal: A diary of things for which you are grateful for, and support you in focusing your attention on positive things. Many successful people including, Oprah, keep a gratitude journal.

- Life Coach: A trustworthy person who is trained in supporting others to reflect on their life experiences by creating a brave space which allows them to talk through their situations while asking thought provoking questions to support them in digging deeper.

- Poetry Journal: Using art to express your true heart is a way to feel what you feel and write it in a way that it can be shared with others without feeling guilty.

- Support Groups: A group of people that come together with common experience or concerns who provide one another with encouragement, comfort, and objective feedback.

These are a few ways, but not all ways you can continue to take inventory. Your willingness and ability to take inventory is directly connected to your success. Continuing these practices will help you cultivate, self-restraint, honestly analyze all situations, and a willingness to admit when you're at fault and willingness to forgive when someone else is at fault.

**Question**

1. What practice or tools will you use to support you in continuing to take inventory?
2. Are you apart of at least one support group? If not, what's holding you back from joining one?

# CHAPTER 11

## Seek

**"Whatever you are looking for you will find. Whatever you are looking for consciously or unconsciously."Jamella Stroud**

You are still in the maintenance phase. In this phase you will continue to live life resisting the temptation of operating in control. You will seek God, or as I call your greater power, through prayer and meditation. This practice will support you in connecting daily with your higher self which will support you in connecting with others.

According to Dictionary.com the word, "seek", means, " to go in search or quest of, to ask for, request, to try to find or discover by searching or questioning." Throughout this process you have been seeking your greater power, God, which is truth. You will continue to look for truth about yourself in belief, thought, feeling and behavior, questioning your motivation, intentions and being clear about them daily. Because the heart can be deceptive at times it's imperative that God, or your greater power, is sought and called upon to support you in searching your heart, mind, soul and spirit.

**Prayer**

Prayer is talking to God, or whomever you call your greater power, and it can looks different for different people. Seeking your greater power, God, through prayer, doesn't mean you have to spend hours on your knees in a closet daily. Prayer can happen at any time of the day and at any place. It's a great practice to set aside a time and place daily for an intentional prayer, and even this can look different for different people. I wake at about 4:30 am every morning. I sit up in my bed or lay down, depending on what I'm feeling that day. Once conscious, I pray sometimes with words out loud and sometimes without words. At night when I journal, my writings are sometimes prayers, where I ask questions about myself and purpose for guidance. I also write prayers of forgiveness and sometimes laments which go through the process of forgiveness.

Lament example from my book, *Bulimic To*

*Believer.*

Lament April 19th 2015:

"Now, Lord, as I sit here in Birmingham at my mother's house, I'm angry and confused, Father. This woman you gave me as a mother, why? Right now I could say some really hurtful things to her because she just said something that was really hurtful to me.

I could say that I never want to see her again, and I really don't like her, and being around her is never a joyous moment for me. She really doesn't understand the impact that she has had on my life, and how I still to this day would like for her to be proud of me. She literally makes me sick at this moment. But You, oh God, knew what I needed to make me who you know I would be. You gave me the "perfect" person to be my mother. Even though I may not see her as being perfect for me, God I believe you see what I need. I write this because as I stood in my mother's room and took my clothes and skirt off to take a bath, she said, "Oh, you need to lose some weight," I asked her, "Why did you say that?" She stated, "Because you have gained weight." Then I reminded her of the time when I first lost weight,

I was really small she told me I was too small I needed to gain weight. For her to tell me now I need to lose weight was very hurtful, because I was confused on what made her say this to me. I'm not overweight at all, so to hear her say that and not have a true concern about my well-being as a person hurt me to the core. Lord, I need to get off this cycle. I felt that I wasn't good enough; as if yet again, I didn't measure up to my mother's standards only to find out I may never measure up to her standards if I was trying to. As a human, her standards are ever changing, but you, oh God, are the only one who is still the same yesterday, today and forever. You are unchangeable and if I behold you as my standards that I should measure to, it will be the same. You are in control of my life and you accept me. I can rest in You and I measure up to Your standards, not man."

You can pray while you're walking, exercising, cooking, do what feels most comfortable you, just be consistent. Consistency supports you in cultivating a connection and conversation with produces a relationship. Prayer is simply put a conversation with God your greater power; you talk, God listens.

**Meditation**

Meditation is listening to God, or your greater power. It increases the awareness of your higher self and God, causing you to be more mindful and conscious of who you are, your beliefs, thoughts, feelings and behavior that impact your success. This is critical to your success because there is a lot of responsibility in being a CEO. There's always something to do as an entrepreneur. With so much to do, it's possible to wake up checking emails, text, social media, or go to sleep with your phone in your hand or laptop in bed. If this is your current reality, your brain is constantly going and going but you're not the Energizer Bunny, you were not created to keep going and going, you will crash, and your crash could send you back to the same mindset and behavior that hindered your success. Meditation supports you in staying grounded.

If you are new to meditation, it may be uncomfortable at first. You may have the urge to move or you may have many thoughts rushing through your head. You may experience thoughts that meditation may feel ineffective, it's not, it's a method you'll have to practice and get better the more you do it. The peace and calmness that you will find from the quiet moments will provide a solace and energy you need to face your daily tasks.

Like prayer, meditation can be different, there is no set way to do it. There are different techniques with the same objective to quiet the mind and listen. When I began to meditate, I followed guidelines from the book *Anatomy of The Soul by* Curt Thompson. In his book, he suggested sitting straight and focusing on an object in the room. Look at the object for thirty seconds then look at another object in the room for thirty seconds then look at another object for 30 seconds repeating this for about three to five minutes, if you're beginning. Doing this helps you focus your attention on the object and nothing else. I would have thoughts that came, and I noticed the thoughts and refocused my attention on the object. I started doing this for five minutes and it was challenging, but I was up for the challenge because I wanted success more and I wanted it without the baggage. From this first meditation technique, I ventured into other meditating methods which were different and longer in time length.

**Meditation Technique**

- Nature: If you are like me and love the great outdoors, you can take a walk outside and pay attention to the birds chirping, the wind blowing, or and literally smelling the warm fragrance of the flowers. This gets you out your head and into your heart in the presence moment. The more connected to the present moment you are, the more at peace you will be and the more connected you will become to your greater power, God.

- Guided Meditation: You can YouTube guided meditation of all kinds for anxiety, stress, and focus, being present with different time lengths and listen to them while sitting still. If you are new to meditation, this can be most challenging because you will be asked to close your eyes, sit or lay still and remain awake and present. There may be a part of you that tells you that you don't have time to meditate or be still because you have to do always be doing something, so allow the thought to be as it is, but resist upon acting on it. There is nothing more important during your meditation time than yourself. I know it can be a difficult belief to accept, but it's true. Your ability to be still impacts your success. Remember mediation is about listening, and the better listener you are the closer you will be with your greater power, God, and your higher self. The closer you are to your higher self your chances of success are greater.

- Art Expression: I'm a writer and it's a part of my meditation. When my pen hits the paper, I am in a zone and become one in that moment, there's nothing more I need, I'm focused, peaceful, calm, and energized during writing. I'm also a dancer. When I dance, I get out my head and into my body and heart allowing my body to move and flow. Dancing gives me great joy as I listen in those moments. I'm able to move through the day and remain attentive to myself and others. Writing and dancing may not be your art or creative form of expression that's meditative for you, it could be painting, singing, drawing, gardening or something else. If you are not sure what it is for you, allow yourself to be free to explore and find it.

Prayer and meditation are essential to your success. How you infuse them into your life is up to you, just make sure you remain consistent when you find the one that works for you.

**Serenity Prayer:**

God, grant me the Serenity

To accept the things I cannot change...
courage to change the things I can,
and wisdom to know the difference.
living one day at a time,
enjoying one moment at a time,
accepting hardship as the pathway to peace.
taking, as He did, this sinful world as it is, Not as I would have it.
Trusting that He will make all things right
if I surrender to His will. That I may be
reasonably happy in this life,
and supremely happy with Him forever in the next. Amen

## Question

1. Are you new to prayer and meditation?
2. Do you think it will be difficult to infuse prayer and meditation into your daily life?

# Chapter 12

## Awakening

**"Awakening begins when a man realizes that he is going nowhere and does not know where to go." ~G. I. Gurdjief**

I can say with confidence that your life and business has changed and shifted in ways you may not be conscious of right now. At the beginning of this book, you were controlling and your unprocessed baggage impeded upon your success and ability to lead efficiently with compassion, understanding, and honesty. If you remember in the second chapter, the imagining exercise, you were in denial, in the raging river, holding onto the tree branch raft. Then you made it to the lake, remained there for some time before you pulled yourself up with the help and support of others while returning to dry land. Now you have reintegrated into society confidence, peace, open hearted and wisdom you are ready servicing others with a newfound perspective, mindset, and heart.

You have experienced a spiritual awakening through these experiences. Your perception of life is different, your response to life, people, and your experiences have shifted. You now realize life is a lesson as some lessons are learned quickly and some slowly, nevertheless, you were willing to learn and grow through all your experiences. A part of you has died, the part that thrives off your inadequacies that's afraid of its shadows and light and something has been replaced. Where there was selfishness, anger, fear, control, now generosity, love, courage, and surrender thrives. You are ready to be a servant leader and share your experience with others. There are others you're connected with in leadership that know you. Other CEO's, COO's, ED's, executive, and leaders that will have an encounter with you, and you'll recognize your old behaviors within them. You will spot the controlling behavior from afar, even if you don't know their full story you will notice and experience their behavior. Don't be alarmed or be off putting, but be patient with them and look for an opportunity to share your process with them. There are many ways to share; Share by telling your story as this allows them to see themselves in your story, or you can suggest this book by telling them you read it and the benefits you received in your life from it. I highly encourage getting involved because there is nothing like giving of your time to support someone else. This could look like finding a mentee and helping them in developing as they enter into the executive and leadership space.

If you haven't already noticed, you will began to practice these steps in every area of your life, family, marriage, business, church and community. The guiding tools you have received will transcend all aspects of your life and the lives of the people you love, lead, and laugh with. Those who work in close proximity with you have already noticed the difference in you. They may not acknowledge or speak it, but they know.

As I wrote this book, I went through this process with intentionality and will to obtain wholeness. I've been on this journey since 2011, and there were still things I needed to confront, feel, and process that caused me to be stuck in control. I incorporated everything I've shared into my own process and probably more because I have a intention to obtain and experience. "Baggage Free Success", which is wholeness. As the book opening quote by Steven Furtick said, "You can have financial success without God, but you can't have significance, there is no significance to any process that God is not the center of. There may be short term success, an illusion of happiness but no deep seated fulfillment in any process where God is not the center." As much as your financial success is important your spiritual, emotional, relational success is equally important. Through this experience and having a spiritual awakening, your spiritual emotional, and relational life have been transformed. From this new place, you will experience true success which will impact your finances and the lives of others for the better as you share your experience with others.

If you question your work and wonder if you have experienced a spiritual awakening, below you will find list to help you realize if you're experiencing a spiritual awakening:

- **Desire to be authentic** - You will have a strong drive pulling you away from people, places, things, and TV shows that do not represent realness. Your higher self will not lie to you. If you find yourself not wanting to hang where you use to and it causes you to not be yourself in those places, this may not be a part of the person you are becoming.

- **Deep yearning for meaning and**

**purpose in life** - Your current title or position with your company may not be fulfilling your purpose. If you find yourself dissatisfied with what your life looks like and you know you have more to offer on the earth, your soul will began to seek out the things that are fulfilling beyond the pay. Allow yourself to explore during this time

- **Deep yearning to connect with others**: You may find that you were once, or are an introvert and satisfied with very little humans interaction. Now you desire to connect with people in an authentic way. You may find yourself looking for groups to be a part of where you can meet people who understand your journey.

- **Hypersensitive**- We are created with five senses: sight, hearing, smelling, touching and tasting. When you experience a spiritual awakening, you become hypersensitive you see beyond what's on the surface of life situations, hear what's not being said, and the ability to touch beyond the physical. Your ability to connect with others emotionally is intensified. You may even experience dreams that are messages for you to understand more about who you are. Ultimately you are able to go deeper, beyond the surface of the five senses into multisensory.

- **Change in sleep patterns**- You may find your body needs more rest than before. If you were a night owl you may find yourself going to bed much earlier and sleeping longer so your body, soul and spirit can come into align. Growth happens while we are sleeping. Your need for more rest is not alarming, allow your body to get what it needs.

- **Transition**- You may experience external transition as you are experiencing internal transition you could leave a job, city, start a business, or a relationship. Your awakening is shifting things within you that also support shift and transition outside of you. Allow yourself to move and feel everything that comes with the transition.

- **Appetite change**- Sometimes you are not eating because you are hungry but because you are feeding something in life such as fear, sadness, anxiety, etc., and these things like junk foods. If you notice you want healthy foods, you are entering into a place of eating for nourishment. Your body knows what it need to support itself in being the best version of itself. Your appetite for better food is a sign of a spiritual awakening.

There are several other signs that signal you are going through, or have experienced a spiritual awakening. Know that your willingness and commitment to you during this process has opened doors for you and you have indeed experienced a spiritual awakening?

**Questions**

1. Have you experienced any of the signs from the list above?
2. If so, which signs have you experienced and what has your experience been like?

# ACKNOWLEDGEMENTS

I would like to say thank you to my Branding Coach Jai Stone for giving me the idea to write this book. In my session with her she helped me pull out things within myself that I knew were there but afraid to say. For this I am grateful. To Lucy Jaffe, facilitator of Women Writing Birmingham, I am forever grateful for your invitation to be a part of this amazing group of women writers. I learned so much about myself and my writing abilities through each woman and the feedback that was shared. To Allison Denise, my business bestie, thank you for your support through the ups and downs of life during this process and life in general. To every staff member at my former company, thank you. It was because of your willingness to work that I was able to learn and grow in so many ways. This book would not be possible without your souls and spirits being a part of my journey, I am grateful for each of you. To my amazing daughter, Jamiah Stroud, I am very proud to be your mother. I am a better person because you chose me to be your guide in the earth. It's because of you that I began writing something that I thought was worth sharing. You are such an amazing and talented young woman and I

## Acknowledgements

know you will obtain baggage free success.

www.ingramcontent.com/pod-product-compliance
Lightning Source LLC
Chambersburg PA
CBHW021441210526
45463CB00002B/605